Amidst the Darkness

Debbie Tosun Kilday

Published by Human Error Publishing

www.humanerrorpublishing.com
paul@humanerrorpublishing.com

Copyright © 2022
by
Human Error Publishing & Debbie Tosun Kilday

All Rights Reserved

ISBN: 978-1--948521-77-2

Cover Design:
Debbie Tosun Kilday - Kilday Krafts

Photography and Artistic Design:
Debbie Tosun Kilday

Editing
Michael L. Kilday

Human Error Publishing asks that no part of this publication be reproduced or transmitted in any form or by any means electronic or mechanical, including photocopy, recording or information storage or retrieval system without permission in writing from Debbie Tosun Kilday and Human Error Publishing. The reasons for this are to help support the publisher and the artists.

"I dedicate this book to all the sad turtles, the ones who give encouragement to others to keep on writing, when they themselves sometimes doubt their own abilities. The ones that dream while awake and see light amidst the darkness"

Table of Contents

Actually	1
A Goddess A Queen	2
A Kiss	3
All the Trauma	4
All Through the Night	5
Alone or Lonely	6
Alone Together	7
A Love	9
A New Generation, A Beat Generation	10
A New Town	12
A River in Winter	13
A Year Had Gone By	14
Beat	17
Castle of Clouds	18
Candy Cane Dreams	19
Choices	20
Compassion	21
Convolution	22
Cuddle Bug	24
Dance	25
Emotions	26
Despair	27
Different Perspectives	28
Does Anyone Care Anymore?	29
Don't Dam Me Up	31
Don't think I'm Invincible	32
Dream	34
Drowning	35
Dry Sockets Flood Waters	36
Farm Life Memories	37
Flying Free	40
Forever	41

Grey Goose	43
Geared	44
He Said He Didn't Lie	45
Hold Tight Forever	46
Hope	47
How do you become a Goddess?	48
I Am A Tree	50
I Am Beat	51
I Am Your Test	53
I I Dream my Life Better	55
Don't Know Anything	57
If I'm a Time Traveler	58
I Flew	60
If You Are Lucky Enough	61
I Found Myself	62
I Like It Sweaty	63
If Love	64
If Only You Knew	65
If You Are Lucky Enough	66
I'm Broken	67
I'm Depressed	68
I'm Just the Cashier	69
I'm Thankful	70
I'm There	71
I Long To Be	72
I Love You Still	73
I Need My Best Friend Now	74
In the Twilight	75
I Remain Alone	76
I Shall Die Of Loneliness	78
I Run My Fingers	79
I Sit Alone	80
It Is	82
It's Fall	84

It's Okay To	85
It Snowed	86
I Wait	88
I Want to Live	89
I was Feeling Kinda Down	90
Just Like	92
Just You	93
Just You and Me	94
Keeping Time	95
Kindness	96
Kindness Not Blindness	97
Last Poet	98
Let Love Reign	99
Live Lovingly Everyday	103
Long Dark Locks	104
Losses	105
Love Flows	106
Loving You	107
Manly Man	108
Maybe	109
Mine is Solitary	110
Mind Body & Soul	112
Mind Travels	113
Misty Musty Night	114
Mold	115
Morning	117
Music, Poetry, Art	118
Mysterious Shadow	119
Nagging Pain	120
Nature Of The Bog	121
None Are	122
No One	124
No Relief	125
Number	126
Number One	127
One Man	130

Ordinary Day	131
Ordinary Woman	132
Our Lives Have Turned	133
Our Two Eyes Met	134
Passion's Muse	135
Pure Bliss	137
Peeling Apart	138
Photographic Dreams	140
Poets are Prisoners	141
Puzzle	142
Queen of the Ballerinas	143
Reluctant Soldier	145
Remember	147
Reminds Me of a Time	148
Revolutionary	149
Roots	151
Sacred	152
Sad Turtle	154
Sadness Runs Deep	155
Scars Unseen	156
Scruffy	159
Sea of Emotions	160
Shoe Whore	161
Show Pony	164
Silly	165
So Much Lost	166
So Wonderful	167
Stressed Heart	168
Take Us Over	169
The Cost	170
The Door	171
The Expression of Me	172
The Forest is Many Things	173
The Pounding Beat	175

The Real Thing	176
The Search for Meaning Starts with You	177
The Silence	178
The Silence Chimed	179
The Sun Shines	181
Thinking Of You	182
Three Trees on the Farmington River	183
Time	184
Tight	186
Today	187
Tragic Artist	189
Travels Through Time	190
Trees	191
Turtle of Despair	192
Two People	193
Under The Stars	195
United	196
When We Were Whole	198
When You Think	201
Who are the Lonely People?	202
Why	203
Worth Expressing	204
You Baby You	205
You Can't Tell Your Heart	206
Your Heart, My Home	207
Your Love Is My Life	208
Your Music Gives Me Life	209
You Ruined Me	210
You Saved Me	211
Yuletide Spirit	212
Bio	213
Books	214
Review	217

Actually

Actually
You never did anything casually
Always loved me passionately

Our meetings, nothing randomly
Always filled with pageantry

Lavishly and elaborately
Showered with fantasy

Bashfully
I fell intellectually
In a tapestry of spirituality
Like from another Galaxy
For you

A Goddess A Queen

As he looked at her
What he saw was a Goddess, a Queen
She was everything
Every man desired

Her lips, as soft as rose petals
Her kiss like thorns piercing his soul

Her eyes, dark as the night
Made his visions & fantasizes
Become realities

The touch of her fingertips
Caused electric sparks to dance across his body
like flecks of light
To bring his mind to ecstasy and flight

She fulfilled every fantasy
Cared for her mans every need

There was one thing overlooked
No man took time to care of her
Her needs were of no importance

She gave him her all
But he did not return her affections
Only taking for his own, her pleasures

One day she was gone
As swiftly as a ravens wings
Never to return

Nurture your Goddess
Or miss her forever

A Kiss

A Kiss
Two Lips
Between Us
= Bliss

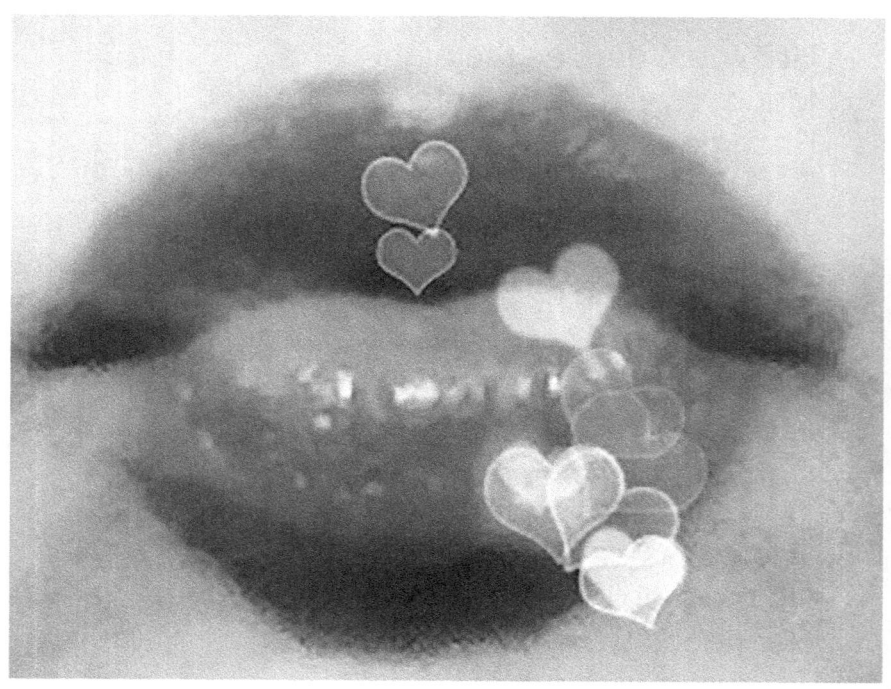

All the Trauma

A darkness falls upon my soul

All the trauma has taken its toll
My only savior is your image
Etched in my mind
Like a game of scrimmage
Soon I will succumb to fate
Found at the floodgate
Like a game of stalemate
Postdated, probated, mutated, orated
Soon to be buried in a hole on the knoll
The reason you ask?

All the trauma has taken its toll

All Through the Night

I want to spoon all night
Have you hold me tight
Give me kisses
All through the night

Alone or Lonely

You may be choosing
To be alone
Living as a hermit

I am alone
Longing for you
I'm lonely

Alone or lonely
It doesn't matter
The outcome is the same

Alone Together

Get me off this pandemic train
The trip seems never-ending

And while there is no stop to get off
I keep seeing ads saying
Alone Together

Can we be both alone and together? I don't think so
I'm trying to keep myself together while alone

I asked myself
Am I alone?
The answer is simple
I always have been

Always on the outside
Not a part of any crowd
Segregated
Bullied

Now in lockdown
In my self-imposed prison
In a single sleeper car
I truly am alone

Are we together?
No. It's not allowed

Together in purpose?
Together as in like minds?

I'd like to think so

But that hope is fading

We haven't been together
For a long, long time
Have we ever truly been together?
When was the last time we boarded the
Peace train

Yes, alone together
We are all alone
We are together as a group alone
On a train to nowhere

The single whistle blows in the distance
As we ride endlessly along the tracks
Alone Together
Alone as One

A Love

A love so intense
I've lost all defense

Can't fight these feelings
My heart is left reeling
For when soul mates meet
Each feels incomplete
Until next they meet
There isn't a quick fix
Being hit by a ton of bricks
The two come undone
Unless merged into one
Hard to understand
Certainly wasn't planned
Looking into your eyes
My soul cries

A love so intense
I've lost all defense

A New Generation, A Beat Generation

Yeah, that's us. A new generation
A Beat Generation
Where did we come from?

It all started when Jack Kerouac
Decided he wasn't following the rules, a sterile set
of sentences created from a set of words and ideas
from someone else's mind.

He wanted his own words, his own ideas, written &
read the way he felt.
He wanted music with his words
There was rhythm but it didn't have to rhyme

We all want the same things
We started out from all different places
All different backgrounds
But we've come together as one
All different, all shades, a beautiful melting of flavors, just like in nature, we are diverse

We are unencumbered by the rules

You have your own form, your own words, your own
style and I'm free to have mine
We are free to be who we want to be

We seem to have some things in common
We speak for those who cannot speak for themselves
People who are put down, poor, forced to do as they
are told, forced to follow traditions that deform &

distort them from how they were born.
Squelched from feeling their own emotions

We speak for our mother, the Earth
The trees, the water, the air we breathe
We fight for a more natural world
With the hope children get to grow up
Without fear of expressing themselves

Yeah, that's us. A new generation
A Beat Generation

A New Town

Sorrow, sadness
Mourning madness
Hearts so heavy
Tearful eyes
Don't dwell on hatred
Stop the madness
Put down the guns
Give only love
Arms only for hugs
Innocent eyes
Hold a future of healing
While honoring their memories
Striving towards a better tomorrow

A River in Winter

Cold and crisp with overtones of grey
Silent in its resting
Yet rushing away to stay moving forward
Looking forward to the change of season
A river in winter waits patiently for change
A river in winter is not unlike you and me
Passive yet actively waiting for spring
Like the river we too wait for the changes
While enjoying our passive rest

A Year Had Gone By

A year had gone by
How time it does fly
Since that terrible car accident
Leaving Mom with head injuries
Unable to work

Leaving me to delay my plans
Of becoming a famous living artist
Painting & Sculpting in Boston, MA

I was only 18 years old
Still believing in dreams
Waiting for my future

Coming home after working
12 hours straight
The house was blaring with noise

Mom? Why is the tv up so loud?
Why is it so hot in here?
It must be 90 degrees

There was no answer
Only noise & heat

In the kitchen
The gas stove
All burners lit
Flames rising up
No pots, just flames

The kitchen sink had a steady stream
Of water pouring down the drain

The washing machine
Water churning without clothing

The sound of the vacuum running
Sitting still on the floor

At that moment my Mom
Rushing towards me
Looking wild eyed & very distraught
Dragging a big black garbage bag
Across the floor

Yelling
Go throw this bag away
And we will all be saved!

Opening the bag
I looked at the contents
Inside all of my belongings

I thought to myself
Did my whole life
Really fit into one garbage bag?

Could the world be saved
If me and my belongings
Were thrown away?

Would my Mom be okay
If I followed her instructions today?

Hello? Operator...
Could you please send an ambulance right away?
What's the problem?
Ummmm.......
I think my Mom just lost her mind
Please hurry

Beat

Has the world beat you up?
Beat you down?
Up, down, all around?
Don't let it
Don't let them
Who is heck is them?
Why, the world of course
The world consists of people
They will tear up up
Tear you down
They will turn you inside out
Upside down
How do I know?
I've been...
Beaten up
Beaten down
Torn up
Torn down
It turned my head around
I've been
Pushed
Shoved
Pulled
Punched
But I must confess
There's no way
It won't happen again
There's a new beat
In town

Castle of Clouds

One of these days when I'm dead
If I'm not dead already
You'll remember
Not the me you forgot, but your Queen
The spicy warm lover of forests
The writer of words capturing your image
My Knight who saved me
Not the me now but the future dead me
Your closest truest friend
Who knew what words would be spoken in silence
For the Knight, beaten down by battle, unable to truly love
Left his Queen
To forever wander through the depths of eternity
There is no pretending to love til you die
Beyond that which is
In the Castle of Clouds

Candy Cane Dreams

Candy cane dreams
Runaway smiles
Brimming faces
Smiling with joy
Holiday scenes
Of stockings & toys
Mittens & scarves
Hot cocoa galore
Candy cane dreams
Come this time of year
Merry times for all
With lots of good cheer

Choices

You made your choices
I'm not to blame for that
I loved you with all my might
You accepted my love
But gave none in return
I tried to hold onto a one way street
But it goes both ways
I made a wrong turn
Now I'm turning around
I'm getting off this dead end
And hopping the freeway

Compassion

Compassion
Reaction
Soul Satisfaction
Give me the tunes
To make my heart soar
To make me capable
To hear others roar
To give of myself

Convolution

Memories try to form
Wrapped around my brain
Curving up
Waiting to spring forth

In a long thin thought
Sequential rings
Try to make a point

My mind, distorted
Pipe dreams
Bend and loop

Tears form on the surface
Of my eyes

My electrical impulses
Are rusty and hollow
I've become empty

Yet like a snake
I coil
Ready to strike

My engine is dead
Twisted and entwined

A sequence of events
Has left me
Spiraling upward
In a cloud of smoke

My mind
Once like clay

No longer flexible
Now stone

Cuddle Bug

Got the cuddle bug
Falling in love
Want to swoon and spoon
Make my heart go zoom
Want to sing a tune
Dance
Play the bassoon
Love bug huddle
Hugging, snuggling
Mumbling and bumbling
Got the cuddle bug
Falling in love

Dance

Dance the midnight dance with me
Bathe in glistening glass sand
Hear the mighty water flow
Kiss the glowing moonlit sky
Caress me with your silken touch

Emotions

Emotions
Get in the way
Loving someone
Being loved
Good times
Bad times
As tears are falling
Hearts are breaking
Emotions
Get in the way

Despair

Despair has come upon me
The void too vast to fill
Contemplating whether or not
To give up or give in
I sit on the edge and wait
Will someone step in and catch me
There is no one it's true
Will someone talk me out of it?
No one to communicate to
My despair is real
There is no doubt
No one knows that better than me
I'm going to the edge right now
No time to hesitate
No one cares or notices
I have now decided my fate

Different Perspectives

You only saw the ocean
From the bow of your boat
You never touched the waters
Where the sand meets the surf
You never felt the rush
As waves hit your body
You call yourself a sailor
Never to experience the beach
It's two different oceans
One in the surf
One from the deck
You're Captain of your vessel
I'm a salty speck
I'd like to take away your boat
For just one day
To let you float in the water
Walk along the beach
To finally experience
The feel of your ocean
At your feet
We both love the ocean
But from different perspectives

Does Anyone Care Anymore?

The words no longer have meaning
They are said out of routine
It hurts to the core
Does anyone, care anymore?

It is shown through actions
Such as kindness, compassion
It seems it's a race
This what seems to be the case

Diligently striving
Crowds shout

Education, equal pay, gay rights,
Homes for the homeless
Feed the hungry

Budget cuts
Keep them out
I want more money
Don't feed the hungry
Dumb them down

It's not okay
What we call today

Love thy neighbor
Do unto others
As you would have them
do unto you

Love
Hate
There's no distinction
It depends on who's listening

Hate

It all depends.
Need money?
Want your neighbor gone?
Fearing rejection?

Love

It won't pay the bills
Fill the stomach
Have someone by your side
If you stand strong, but alone

The words no longer have meaning
They are said out of routine
It hurts to the core
Does anyone, care anymore?

Don't Dam Me Up

Drawn by the current
Driven by desire
Don't dam me up
Let me flow freely in all directions
To give life to my many expressions
Let the force within
Surface to the top
Silently the rage is just beneath the waves
Hoping to burst forth at any moment
Don't dam me up

Don't Damn Me Up

Drawn by the current
Driven by desire
Don't damn me up
Let me flow freely in all directions
To give life to my many expressions
Let the force within
Surface to the top
Silently the rage is just beneath the waves
Hoping to burst forth at any moment
Don't damn me up

Don't think I'm Invincible

Don't think I'm invincible
I'm not
I try to bend
But if pushed
I'll break into pieces
I have withdrawn
Into a voided world
It's lonely there
It feels like snowflakes
 Shards that disappear
I'm there one minute
But if driven to the edge
I'll fall and melt into nothing
I scatter myself in all directions
Trying to find reason
But nothing makes sense
What remains are fragments
Of what I once was

Dream

Dreaming of a time
In your embrace

Lovingly looking
Into your soul

Through eyes
Shining wide and bright

Happiness, laughing
Playfully touching

Fingertips pressed
Hands grabbing

Holding closely
To dreams

This time may pass
To memory

Unfulfilled destiny
Held close in heart

Dreams are dreaming
Hoping to become reality

Dreams are memory
Of things now dreamt

Reality is hope
Dreams take flight
Today

Drowning

Loneliness
Rips at the heart
Like broken chards of glass

As a lonesome traveler roams
without a destination

An artist struggles to create
Without canvas, paint, or brushes

A hiker is lost in the wilderness
With no search & rescue

The burdens of life
Bring frozen tears
That melt into quicksand

I'm drowning

Dry Sockets Flood Waters

Eyes sore
Open so long
They want to rest
Tears flowed
Rubbed them raw
Sockets are sandy
Eyes to cry
Flood waters
Lubricate all
Troubles washed
Seeing clearly now

Farm Life Memories

It was life, real life, amongst the willows by the pond, on the farm

It wasn't about money or things

It was about loving the earth under your nails
Loving animals you cared for

Cooperation was abundant, everyone helped each other

There was no time to waste; there was a job for everyone

In return you were provided milk, eggs, veggies, clean air, and water

I remember gathering the eggs, milking the cows, planting the seeds

Grey goose was our watchdog, Queenie, our Collie dog, my best friend.

My playground was Nature:

Watching peep toads, catching fireflies, making dinnerware out of clay

It was life, real life, amongst the willows by the pond, on the farm

I miss it

Flying Free

While walking along
Winding trails of green
Sifting through
Gardens in full bloom
Brushing against my cheek
A buttery figure flew by
Sun shone through
Stained glass paper wings
In shades blue, yellow & grey
Landing on a flower
With petals of crimson red
Wandering mind
Imagining myself
Unencumbered
Flying free
Sipping nectars
Like fine wines
Flittering along
With no cares
Flying free

Forever

I lay here in my bed, alone in silence

It's agonizing, yet I wait.
Why is there no call, no form of communication, to express your loss of me?

In the midst of my life you said you wanted only me.
Yet you always had someone else to build a series of life's expressions with.

I never knew what the attraction was.
Why we decided to be something; friends, lovers, professing our love.
We were more than that, yet never anything permanent.

At each meeting we were limited.
You always had to return to another life, another partner.
Time was always punishing us.

You couldn't be late for them; never disappointing someone else.
I always wished it would be us; living a life filled with experiences, not just a few hours of pure bliss.

You changed partners several times, never wanting us full-time.
I was always waiting in the wings hoping for that moment; where you would tell me we would be together.

But the cruel hands of the clock always whisked you away to another.
I wasn't enough to fulfill you, not then, not now.
Driven to feel so utterly hopeless,
restless yet resigned, finally ending us, me, life.

Forever: alone in my bed for all eternity.

Grey Goose

Grey Goose's southern comfort seduces me as he takes flight
To faraway places dark into the night

Not native to these parts
He shows me the fine art of playing the ace of hearts

His eloquent feathers take me under his wing
Making my heart sing as if in a fairies ring

Grey Goose's southern comfort seduces me as he takes flight
To faraway places into the night

Geared

My gears are stuck
They used to turn
Motioning effortlessly
Around in spirals
Almost out of control

My pocket watch
Fell off its chain
Causing it to roll
Into the 20th century

My rose colored goggles
Got stuck in my cascading curls
Which tipped my bowler hat

I tripped on my long Victorian skirt
While looking for my walking stick

I'm a retro mechanical, high heeled, buckle strapped, boot wearing, post apocalyptic, futuristic, twisted, steam punk mess

He Said He Didn't Lie

He said he didn't lie
But he did

About everything

He said he loved only me
While texting another goodnight

He planned a future for us
Only I was not included

He shared his secrets
Except the ones kept from me

He said I was the only one for him
Yet he spent his free time with others

He lied and cheated
Hurt many including me

That's the only truth left between us

He said he didn't lie
Which was a lie

Hold Tight Forever

When meeting for the first time
Yet feeling a familiarity
With eyes sultry yet smiling
You looked into my soul
Reached in without hesitation
Grabbed hold of my essence
Never to let go

Friendships form in
Most peculiar ways
Or was it meant all along
That my heart be held
With such a force
Never beating for anyone else

Whatever it is
Whatever it feels like
It cannot be ignored

Instead of relishing in bliss
Heartache
Separated by distance
Circumstances
Responsibilities

Yet you never let go
Once you reached in
Grabbing my soul
Please don't ever
Hold tight forever

Hope

Life lost
Love lost
Sorrow abounds
Yet
Hope makes the world go on

9/11 is a date never to be forgotten
Yet
Our hearts ache
For those souls lost and found

We are all connected
To that thin thread called life & death

Life lost
Love lost
Sorrow abounds
Yet
There is hope for the future
That makes the world go on

How do you become a Goddess?

How do you recognize one?
Is it seen?
Touched?
Felt?
Is it a state of being?

Is it something that you work to become?
Is there a test?
Some unknown knowledge

To me it is simple
You live and breathe in kindness
Compassion is shown to all
You care for others
Not only yourself

You hear the cries of the hungry
You shelter those that are without
You hear with your heart
You do no harm

To recognize a Goddess
You must be one

It's a coming together
There is no gender
It's a melding of colors
Yet you see none

As we gather today
In our virtual socially distanced world
Our beauty is in our actions

Our voices are heard and felt
We celebrate each other
We vibrate love
Love cures all the ills that ail us

Welcome Goddesses
Today we celebrate each and everyone

I Am A Tree

I've grown from a single seed
Spread my branches
Reached for the stars
Meditated on the moments

Deep far reaching roots
Dug into the soil tell my age

My wish is to continue
Wishing upon a star
Making dreams come true
Bathing in the sun
Shedding my bark
Scattering leaves
Making a home for many
Inciting inspiration to poets lips

I am a tree
But more than that
I symbolize life in progress

I Am Beat

I must admit
I am beat

Beaten down by experience
Smashed to bits
Ground down
By pestle and mortar

Made into a chalky paste
Like pesto
Without the pine

An empty cone
Of intricate webs

A cocoon
Turned to stone

There is no escape
Only hope

That the layers
That peel off
My parchment

Do not take me down
Kerouac Lane
Left to howl
At a generation
Beaten down and poor

But made renewed
Sympathetic
Pure
As was intended

A new generation
Forged from stones
But crushed into clay

Made pliable
Ready for change

Sculpted from ashes
Rising up
In waves

Renewed by waters
A jazzy ensemble
Pounding to the beat

I Am Your Test

We met out of the blue or so you thought
Nothing in common you became distraught
Wanting to show Me "The Way"
Told me how Jesus had saved you from going astray
How Jesus would save me too
You were not sent to me
I was sent to you
I am YOUR test
How you perceive me is your test
Will you step up to the quest?
 Embrace me or turn away?
Thinking I deserve pain will you run away?
Will my pain be yours?
It's your turn to do the right thing
Will you repeat your ways as in the old days?
Will you embrace me and show me compassion?
Or leave me to die saying
I died for your transgressions
I was your savior then as I am now
Will you follow me, with those who are without?
Or will you follow the crowds who are always in doubt?
Are your riches within or only outwardly displayed?
Pass my test and I will show You "The Way"
I am YOUR test

I Dream my Life Better

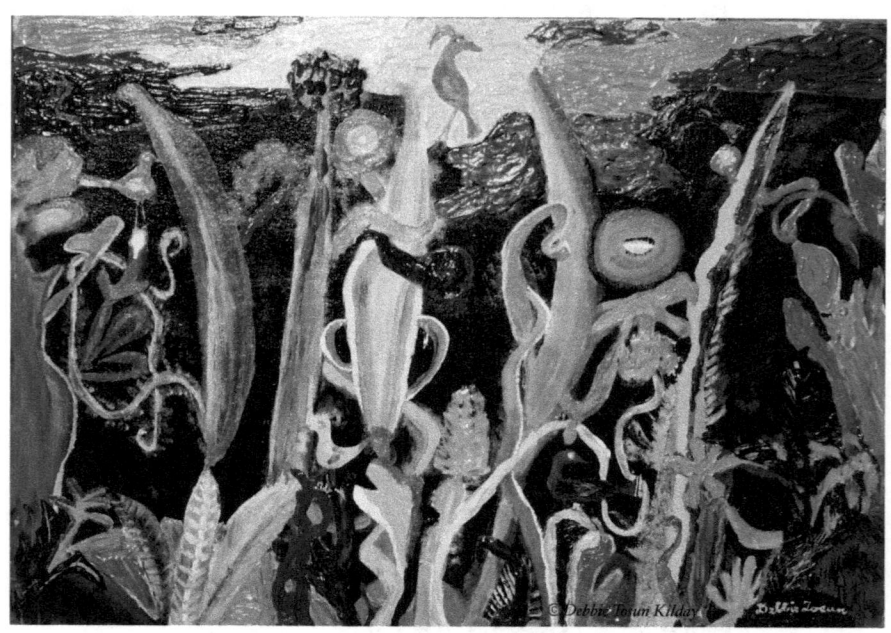

I sometimes think I dream my life
better than I live it.

In my dreams

I run barefoot through fields of green grass
after a summer rain.
The fact that I am running at all
makes me realize it's a dream.

In my dreams

I hear the birds chirping songs
so sweet it is a symphony to my ears.
Awake I realize I hardly hear the songs of birds
these days. There are so few.

In my dreams

I ramble through never-ending forests.
The trees hold out their branches to embrace me. I climb up to view the world from up above.
I never feel alone.

When awake the clear cut reality is the forests are no more. The landscape is bare.

In my dreams

The skies are blue and the waters run clear and pure.
I awake to the dreary grey day and must filter my water before drinking.

In my dreams

I live in peace and harmony.
I awaken to arguments and I must flee for safety.
But sometimes I think I may someday live my life as beautiful as my dreams.
There was a time I lived my life better than my dreams.

So I hold onto my dreams and try to live them into a new reality.

I Don't Know Anything

I don't know anything
It's just something left to do

If I'm a Time Traveler

If I'm a time traveler
A passenger in a lackluster 7th dimension
Then I want to be wrapped in silken ropes
Like a falconers strings
Entwining our bodies together
Putting no limits on our love

So that each time we meet
Time soars in flight
Floating and swaying to the beat

I Flew

The driving rain
A passenger train
They all remind me of you
I hopped a plane
To Key Biscayne
That's all I thought to do
It's been awhile
Since seeing you
It's very hard to do
To be away
From loving you
Takes all my strength
It's true
As I walked to the door
And knocked
I almost turned
And walked
You opening the door
Is the stuff of lore
Seeing me there
You showed you care
Into your open arms
I flew

If You Are Lucky Enough

If you are lucky enough

To have love offered
Love is such a rare gift
Don't hesitate to accept
It is never too late to appreciate
Grab love freely
Give love with all your passion
What you will gain is love
Nothing more, nothing less
The greatest of gifts

If you are lucky enough

I Found Myself

I found myself
Like an elf felting a shoe
In the middle of a field
In grass as tall as a tree
You see, my world starts from below
Closest to earth
A kindred soul
To all that came before me
A couple of times I grew ten feet tall
Only to fall upon a rain bow
I found myself
Just like a troll
Digging in dirt
Thou I must admit
I must divert
The lungwort that surrounds me
You see, my world starts from below
Closest to earth
A kindred soul to all who know me

I Like It Sweaty

Working outside, earth in my hands
Droplets of water pouring off my skin
I like it sweaty
Packing up to move to a new location
Seeing the super heated water
Rising out of my pores
I like it sweaty
Lying in the midday sun salty
and hot after running in the ocean
I like it sweaty
Making love all night long
as if in a marathon
I like it sweaty

If Love

If Love is the opposite of hatred
If Love shows respect and friendship

Let's choose Love

If Kindness is the opposite of cruelty
If Kindness melts hard hearts

Let's choose Kindness

If Compassion is the opposite of tyranny
If Compassion brings understanding

Let's choose Compassion

If Love is all there is

Let's show it
Let's do that

Let's choose Love

If Only You Knew

If only you knew
The profound love
I have for you
It's not to be ignored
Or avoided
Nor scorned
If only you knew
How my heart aches for you
If only you knew that
I love only you

If You Are Lucky Enough

If you are lucky enough

To have love offered
Love is such a rare gift
Don't hesitate to accept
It is never too late to appreciate
Grab love freely
Give love with all your passion
What you will gain is love
Nothing more, nothing less
The greatest of gifts

If you are lucky enough

I'm Broken

I'm broken
But you can't see it
Not an arm or leg
Not a tooth or nail
That would be visible
I'm broken
But you can't see it
It's my heart
My spirit
It's hard to fix those
They may not be repairable
I'm broken
But you can't see it
Look into my eyes
My spirit is dimmed
Feel my heart
It beats irregularly
I'm broken
But you can't fix that
Only love can fix that

I'm Depressed

I'm depressed
Showing signs of distress

Can't seem to rest
Haven't even got dressed

A chilling image
Signs of slippage

Physical damage
Couldn't manage

Ravaged, hopeless
Can't focus

Turning away
Those closest

Fighting demons
Feeling like screaming

No reason
It's rainy season

There is no other
Way of conveying

So I'm just saying
I'm depressed

I'm Just the Cashier

I'm just the cashier
I sit on my derriere
I watch the faces
Of people passing by
Some struggling to find change
Both in life, and coin
I'm just the cashier

I'm Thankful

I'm thankful
To have you in my life

Although not together
A part of my heart

In my mind
Your gentle touch
Kindred soul

A part of me
Only you possess

I'm thankful
For you

I'm There

From the depths of despair
Liquid trust

Drowning in olives
A must

Numb from all worries
Exempt from responsibilities

No hope of repair
Not wishing I'm here

I Long To Be

I long to be
Wrapped in your arms
For all eternity

I Love You Still

I love you still
Only you
No one else will do

You make me fly
Like a caged bird set to flight

My heart flutters
With wings
Brought to new heights

Submitting to your will
Bending to your ways
Dominated by your spell

Subdued by your touch
Mesmerized by your kiss

My flesh surrenders
Bound to you
Suggestive of

A free flying dove
Feathering your body
Nesting in like a glove

We dance
In love

I love you still

I Need My Best Friend Now

I need my best friend now
The one I was always there for
To convey my feelings to
To heal my broken heart
To hold me tight all night
To listen without interruption
To wipe away my tears
I need my best friend now
Where are you?

In the Twilight

In the twilight I see shadows
Of a past life not yet lived

In the twilight there is no darkness
Only light subdued by grey

In the twilight I can't see clearly
For I have lost my way

In the twilight I feel comforted
For my flaws cannot be seen

In the twilight I see hope
For the time has come

To start a new day
Day is dawning
The sun is about to warm me

I can see my shadow
The light shows me the way
To a brighter future
Well lived

I Remain Alone

Longing for your affection
My body aches
For fear of rejection
I remain alone

My mind envisions
You holding me
Safely I relax
Caressed in your arms
Holding me tight
My mind
Starts to wander
With thoughts
Of desire
My passion
Unites with yours
Our flames burn
White hot

Longing for your affection
My body aches
For fear of rejection
I remain alone

I Shall Die Of Loneliness

I shall die of loneliness
A solitary emptiness not by choice

Prone to be alone
I won't make it on my own

I shall die of loneliness
A solitary emptiness not by choice

No one to tell things to
No one to compel me to go on

I shall die of loneliness
A solitary emptiness not by choice

No one to notice me
Feeling hopeless as can be

I shall die of loneliness
A solitary emptiness not by choice

I Run My Fingers

I run my fingers
Through your hair
Along your brow
Down your cheek
Across your back
As I do, I feel your pulse
Your heart starts to race
I run my fingers
Up and over your backside
Between your legs
Down your calves
Caressing your ankles
Touching your toes
As I do, I feel your pulse
Your heart pounds
I run my fingers

I Sit Alone

I sit alone in an upstairs room
The only company I have are my thoughts

Feelings of sorrow pass over me
As I try to hold back the tears

Thinking of happier times when I had someone who seemed to love me
Only to leave me for a more exciting and younger version of myself
At least that's what I imagine to be the reason

I sit in a comfortable cushioned chair
Looking out the multi paned window
Overlooking the landscape

I see the sunlight filtering through the trees
The river moves slowly in the background

It is winter
A time when things die off
Just as my relationship had come to an end

It's been years since he first kissed me
On the banks of the same river
Only a few miles downstream from here

He told me then he wanted only me
Would never love another
And made me promise to stay with him forever

I promised him

But now I realize his promise and words were empty
He would leave me when a better option came along
That time had come now

Some would say years of love is something to be treasured
But the same years now are viewed as wasted energy
On someone who did not know the true meaning of love

The sun is now starting to fade
As day turns to night

I came to this place to escape my loneliness
Only to feel utterly alone and helpless
My thoughts are my only companion

It Is

It Is
Fluidic
Shapeless
Smooth -or- Rough
Illusive

It Is
Soft -or- Hard
Responsive
Prismatic
Reflective -or- Shiny
Non-Organic
Edible
Emotional
Influencing
Wet
Absorbent
Conductive
Ever-Moving
Material

It Is
Non-Living
(It is not alive, and is/was never alive, so it can also not be dead).

It Is
A Medium

It Is
Smothering.
Yes, It can smother you, cut off your oxygen,

and drown you.
But given proper respect & care, it will give you precious life and sustain you.

It's Love in the purest form

Water!

You need to protect it at all cost
It is not a peaceful demonstration
It is life! Your life! My life! Our life!

Water is life!
It Is!

It's Fall

A chill is in the air
Pumpkins Making faces
Leaves Blushing
Temperatures Dropping
Flowers Wilting
Squirrels Gathering

Dance Around the campfire
Eat an apple pie
Wear your checkered red shirt
There is nothing
So wondrous
It's Fall

It's Okay To

It's okay
It's okay to cry, feel sadness, and loss
I have stained many a pillow with my tears
Don't ever let anyone else tell you why you shouldn't
It's your sadness, not theirs
No need to explain it
Can't just Feng Shui it away

It Snowed

It snowed
But it was already cold
Inside, the tendrils of ice
Wrapping your heart
Surrounded me

Making me stiff
Without emotions
Devoid of empathy
Just as you
Showed none to me

After years of struggling
Trying to break free
Of your grasp
Stifling any emotions

Finally free
Just as the turtle
Cut from the ropes
Of the fisherman's net

Rushing back to sea
Flying through currents
To a place of safety

Reflecting back
I see there are places
That melt human suffering
Bringing erratic hearts
To a steady beat

Finding solace
In the fact
There is hope
After the snow melts

I Wait

I wait
Screaming yet silence
Inside a trance state
I wait
Standing still
While Dancing
I wait
The phone rings
The doorbell dings
I wait
Without reason
Thinking sensibly
I wait
Beyond reach
Grabbing hold
I wait

I Want to Live

I want to live
Not just survive
Let me live
Let me ride
I want to live
Not just survive
Up on the hilltops
Far and wide
Don't get me off
This roller coaster ride
I want to live
Not just survive
If I can't
I won't survive
Then off to the rooftop
To take a dive
I want to live
Not just survive

I was Feeling Kinda Down

I Was Feeling Kinda Down
2 O'clock
You figure out
If it was am or pm

I got up, showered, dressed
Slathered on some makeup
It wasn't pretty
You could still see my tears stains beneath
Looking like rain drops
Only more like icicles hanging off a roof

The layers I pan caked on
Stood on the surface of my skin
Giving it an eerie glow

My clothes didn't quite shift into place
Making me look lopsided
As I walked, my gait was zombie..ish

I was really low
So low, I couldn't have dug much deeper
Graves are much shallower than this

I should be rejoicing
I should be smiling
But alone I'm desolate
My heart aches

Did you know you can die from a broken heart?
If that's true I'm dead already
That could explain it

Looking in a mirror there wasn't a reflection
Just a memory of past lives
Happier times… with people
Conversations, sharing meals, loving life
Now all is empty

There is nothing left to say
No one to share with
My heart no longer beats for anyone

The sheer magnitude of this quake
Shook me to my core
Crumbling me up into a bag of bones

Cause of death?
No hope

Just Like

I want you
You want me

I flaunt it
You want it

I'm your debutante
You're my commandant

You wooed me
In lieu of just Phillips screwing me

You knew me
You subdued me

You slew me
Looked right through me
You viewed the true me

You ballyhooed
I mewed
We hullabalooed

Out of the blue
Just like mulligan stew

We lag screwed
Must be long overdue
Déjà vu

Just You

Don't need diamonds
Only the sparkle in your eyes

Don't need money
Just for you to be my honey

Wouldn't trade you
For all the riches of the world

Just hold me tight
All through the night

Don't be afraid
Just call me your Babe

Just You and Me

Just you and me
Wrapped up in love
Looking pretty as can be
Every day of my life
The girl within me
The expression of life
If you think you could
Love someone like me
Come take me in your arms
Make sweet love to me
For no better time
Then right now will be
The time for us
Just you and me

Keeping Time

Ding, dong. Ding, dong...
Ding, dong. Ding, dong...

Dong... dong... dong...
Cuckoo, cuckoo, cuckoo.
Tick tock, tick tock, tick tock.

Will it not stop?
The incessant Tick Tock?
The hands of the clock?

They would not rest.
As if a test
So extreme it seemed.

I listened and waited
Some were silent, yet...

It flew by
Faster than a fly
I got no shut eye

In the end, what I found,
Quite simple, yet profound,

Time waits for no one.
It never stood still.
I lost it, never to regain it.

Buzzzzzzzzzzzzzzzz.
Snooze...
Repeat.
TIME... to get up!
What time is it?

Kindness

Kindness is underrated

A timeless warm-hearted act
Giving a hug
Holding a hand
Smiling
Listening
Human and sympathetic
A forgiving tendency
Never to be ignored

Kindness is underrated

Kindness Not Blindness

Kindness not blindness

Don't turn away
Look me in the eyes
You've side glanced me for too long
You think you won't hurt if you don't
Your inability to see
The hurt you created for me
Leads to more blindness

Kindness not blindness

The only way you'll see
The kindness from me

Last Poet

The last Poet has died
Or have they?

I hear a voice
It calls to me
It's one of many voices

I hear the words
Still relevant today
As they were then

Thoughts and ideas
cannot be silenced
No one can erase their mark

I'll use my voice and be heard
Just as those before me

Voices no longer heard
Are etched in our hearts

Today it's our turn
Speak up Poet

We fight for the good
We matter
Without our words
There is no hope
Without hope there are no words

There is no last Poet
We keep recycling
I am just the first to speak
Then it's your turn

Let Love Reign

The world was filled with green
Music of birds was the theme
The skies were blue
Trees were sacred beings
Animals roamed freely
Natural selection was the rule

Until that first shot
Turned the skies from blue to red
BANG!
It zoomed through the air
A shower of rain made of metal
A device so cold
It had no specific target
Indiscriminately it sought its victims
There was no close contact
It didn't see their eyes
It didn't feel the breath leaving them
There was no self defense
It only brought death
Destruction
Sadness
Loss

Randomly it hit the innocent
The guilty
The children
None were ready to succumb
To its violent fire
The burning strike of death
The piercing bullet
Draining their life

Nothing was left but the empty shells
The broken skin
The oozing blood
From the heap of cold colorless flesh

Who do you blame for these happenings?
What type of being kills without conscious
Why have these happenings
Been accepted?
Why are we numb to it?
Who fights for continued violence?

I continue to ask these questions
One victim at a time

What beauty do people see
When choosing a gun?
Or any weapon?

How do you justify an instrument of death
As being your brand new toy
or your companion
Or your feeling of security

Most won't listen to my words
My words are plain
They have no flair
They are a plea for sanity and reason

But people are well conditioned
To believe in the idea of
Kill or be killed
If someone is different than you
Fear rules their hearts

So they act cowardly

I remember from a past life
A young man speaking his words
Sharing his truth
He was one of the earliest victims
Only to be dragged, beaten,
and tied to a cross made of wood
Left to die
Wounded
Bleeding

He then became a symbol
An excuse
To not take responsibility for your own actions

The lie was compounded by saying he died for your sins

As if it was his choice
For all of humanity to believe and perpetuate the lies and deception

So that others could continue
To destroy, mame, rape, and kill

In modern times we have continued
To destroy our own societies
Our own families
We keep finding excuses
We pray for the victims we kill.

I meditate with my actions
I breathe in the air

I worship my home the Earth
She is my symbol
Of everlasting life
I preach peace, love, kindness
Heed my words
They bring gentler times
Teach acceptance of our differences
But make an effort to do no harm

Let Love rain upon you
Instead of bullets

Live Lovingly Everyday

Uninterruptedly
Live lovingly

Warmly
Speak softly

Charmingly
Do no harm

Without enticements
Show acts of kindness

Live Lovingly Everyday

Long Dark Locks

My long dark locks flow down below my waist
They are strong and resilient just as I am
Twirling them around my finger in repetition
Separating them into three strands I braid them one layer at a time
Working the suds and water through with my fingers
Letting the air dry them naturally
Brushing them to one side in long wide strokes
At other times flinging them over my shoulder
They blow in the breeze while riding in my car
Never to be restrained only to flow free just as I long to be

Losses

We all have losses
Today is no different
Don't we lose a little fragment of ourselves,
Inside the workings of our bones?
Don't we excrete tears?
Are we not biting our nails in despair?
I seem to remember reading a book
About the functions of the human body
It was given to me by my mother
Who thought I needed to know this knowledge.
She feared I wouldn't know how to walk
Or why you run
I read the part that described chewing
And thought about when I bit my tongue
While chewing a piece of gum

Love Flows

Love flows from my heart and soul
Never-ending tides of emotion take their toll
Strong willed waves drown me in passion
Flowing in and out effortlessly, our rhythm's as one
One gives, one takes, without reaction
Separate yet connected we run the same course
Like racing waters meeting at the dam
Love flows from my heart and soul
The river rages to meet with passionate tides
Our flow of love runs smoothly
Clashing together like waves against the rocks
Yet gentle in the stillness of desire
Love flows from my heart and soul

Loving You

Loving you
Is all I want to do
It's an easy task
With you

Each day
An adventure
Each night
A pleasure

Loving you
Seemed easy
To keep your love
Very hard

Time slips by
There is no rewind
No do-overs
No second chance

Loving you
Is all I want to do
Loving me
Is all I want from you

Manly Man

Manly man

Don't try to control me
Dominate over me
Show me your passion
Let it take us over
Let us fly into the night sky

Manly man

Bring me to new heights
Bathe our desires
Show your strength
Wrap me in your arms
Hold me tight
Kiss me with all your might

Manly man

Have the courage to love

Maybe

Maybe one day I'll be your desire
We'll walk hand and hand
Be immersed in our flame of fire

Maybe one day we will dress in our finest attire
Go out on the town
Dancing til dawn

Maybe that day will never transpire
Maybe one day you won't be a liar

Mine is Solitary

Everyone knows who I am,
What I do, where I've been.
They think they have ME all figured out.
I read somewhere where I would be going next.
I'll let you in on a little secret.
I don't know who the fuck I am
I don't know where I'm going
I'm not completely sure where I've been
And what is IT exactly,,, what is IT that I do?

Whatever IT is that I do
I do very well. I can tell you that.
One thing for certain
There's no denying
My depression is solitary
No one knows but me
That place, that place that defines

Who I really am.
If you trace back from where I am now,
to where I was then.
What you'll find is a public figure
Who has my name, my looks, my demeanor.
But that's not me.
My depression is solitary
There is where you'll find the real me.

Mind Body & Soul

The whole person is what I wanted
Intrigued by your ability to think and discern what others could not
You moved with a savory gait that made me want you
The aura of your soul shown bright when you walked into the room

Mind, Body & Soul

We meshed on an intellectual level others couldn't understand
Our two bodies fit perfectly like two puzzle pieces fused together
Our souls recognized each other in spirit

Mind, Body & Soul

Mind Travels

Sleepless nights
Walking beaches
Sands are seamless
Waves seem endless
Pieces of shells
Fragments beneath the ocean floor
Where my mind wanders like waters lost

Misty Musty Night

Dark, dank
Misty, musty, night
There was nothing to do
Lest muster up a fright
A fright so frightening
It would make your flesh crawl
Make your eyes pop
Make you curl up into a ball
Dark, dank
Misty, musty, night
Green ghouls rising
Lost souls surprising
Dark, dank
Misty, musty, night
There was nothing to do
Lest muster up a fright

Mold

You tried to mold me
Into something I never was

I would never be
What you wanted

You see, it is simple
I give love
I accept love
I'm all about love and loving

You are all about control
Made me feel
That I could never be
What you wanted

I just wanted to touch you
Caress and care for you

I would never be controlled
Or beg for your attention

Let me be free
I can't be bound
To all your rules
Never to just
Accept me
For the woman I am

Why would you refuse a pure love
Without limitations
I don't understand it or you

I'm a free spirit
My wings must be free to fly
To soar above

Morning

Morning is a reminder
The creation of a new day
A new chance
To be grateful & kind

Yet restless
Restless for change

Not wanting to repeat
The mistakes
Of the past

Reflecting
Then discarding
The poisons
Injected by
Those who
Take prisoners

Only to discard
The many hearts
Who fell victim
To the deception

Music, Poetry, Art

Music, poetry, and art, is for keeping us moving forward and finding ways of bringing us together.

We are able to find beauty in darkness.
We create light from the burning shadows.
We embrace the fight for the good of all.

We overcome those who try to destroy our freedoms.
Our voices are heard through the echoes of time.
Music soothes our souls even when shattered. Even those who cannot hear can feel the beat.

Poetry brings our words to the masses. We express our words in different ways so all can hear.

Art is a part of the visions we see in our minds, then transferred to touch our hearts.

We are a new generation of Beats. We speak through the arts.

Our music, words, art, we dance while moving forward.

Our only weapons are our minds, our words, our own creations.
We are Artists in every sense of the word.
We are the Beats.

Mysterious Shadow

A mysterious shadow appeared
As fog lifted to the heavens
As sunlight disappeared into the depths
Only despair and darkness filtered through
We are to die as much as we are to be born
There is no delaying the fascination we have
With death nor the joy of birth
The two both share a beginning and end

Nagging Pain

Tears are falling
Harder than the rain
All I'm feeling
Is a nagging pain
Missing you
Oh so much
Longing for
Your gentle touch
Kissing my lips
Caressing my brow
Wishing you were
With me now
Tears are falling
Harder than the rain
Love feeling happy
Not riddled with pain
True love had come
Now it's gone
Gotta press on
Not be withdrawn
Tears are falling
Harder than the rain
All that remains
Is this nagging pain

Nature Of The Bog

Looking for words
Spurred the greatest ever heard
The songs of
Red winged blackbirds
Garter snakes slithering
Through the Sphagnum peat moss
In hope of catching a Lemming
Hiding in myrtle bogs
The Pitcher plant & Sundew
Fighting to devour
A hungry mosquito
Dragonflies and Mayflies
Do an aerial dance
While the tiny bog turtle
Does flip dives
Through the acidic water
High Bush blueberries, cranberries
Labrador for Tisane tea
Such a treat for us humans
Dark, dank brown muddy water
Still brimming with life
Nature in full splendor

None Are

None of the dead are among us
None have or will return

None of those taken from us
Can support one platform or another
Just be lost to those that mourn

They can just rot amongst the others
Be a memory of what violence brings

Don't support that
Which instills more fear

Violence being supported by more violence
Is not a cure

Teaching non-violence
Will teach no weapons are needed

There is no justification
For a world depleted

Why would anyone want to arm the world with weapons
When we could spread peace
And let the killing crease

Love is the answer
Killing on either side
Just brings more death

More joy is needed

Not more mourning

Statistics show no life
Among the dead

No One

No one said it would be easy
No one promised you success
If you were to remember
No one really could care less

There weren't any hints
Or instruction manual
On what to do
For a semblance of a life
All you had was a made-up promise
That you would be alright

Your first mistake was trusting
What others told you to be true
Especially when they too
Had no clue as what to do

You see no life comes with instructions
No one else can predict
For what it all comes down to
Is you trusting the voice inside your head

Only you can run your life
Fail miserably on first tries
Learn lessons as you go along
And if you're lucky
Survive

No Relief

There is no relief
In this sweltering heat
Out walking the streets
Getting something to eat

There's no rhyme or reason
This is the season
I knew right from the start
We should never part

Life got in the way
Then you couldn't stay
So to my disbelief
Bewildered with grief

I remain with you
In my heart
Like a memory of fine art
But still apart with

No relief

Number

1-800-273-TALK(8255)
1-800-273-TALK(8255)
1-800-273-TALK(8255)
Why are people giving me this number?
Do I look emotionally distressed?
Does my appearance show me as suicidal or in a crisis?
Do I look like someone who might want to kill themselves?
Was it something I said?
It seems odd that I was just thinking to myself how I could do it; kill myself, and not be able to undo it if I had the nerve to go through with it in the first place. Did someone hear my thoughts? I hope not. I don't want anyone to know. The story is so tragic.
I would go walking along the river, lose my footing on the slippery moss covered rocks, and be swept under by the strong current. No one would suspect a thing. The rocks were slippery, I didn't know how to swim, I didn't realize the danger. No one was to blame. It was just an accident. The poor thing never had a chance.

The National Suicide Prevention Lifeline (1- 800-273-TALK [8255]) It provides a 24/7, toll-free hotline available to anyone in suicidal crisis or emotional distress.

What a nice day for a walk along the river.

Number One

At first
I never realized
I was different
Not accepted

It seemed to happen
For others, not me
Never treated special
Sitting on the sidelines

Waiting on the phone line
Cuz an important call came in
Pushed into the corner
As if I didn't matter

At the end of the buffet
Only leftovers, stale with time
Got asked on a date
As a last minute choice

As years went by
I stepped aside
I learned to hang up
Waited to get served

Opened my own doors
Put my own coat on
Treated as second best
Was the norm

A fill in date
If someone else cancelled

I settled as second best
Accepted my position

Alone, ignored
I was no one's
Not number one
Not even a close second

At first
I never realized
How could I recognize
Something never seen

You put me first
I didn't know the feeling
Didn't ever imagine
I'd find myself on the A list

It happened quite unexpectedly
Took me by surprise
You let me go first
Ahead of the rest

First and foremost
Front and center
Told the others
They had to hold on

You ran around the car
To hold my door open
You held my coat
While I put it on

For once in my life
I was first
Someone's number one
Your one and only

You held me close
Never let me feel alone
It was then I knew
You're my number one too

One Man

One man's love is all you need
One man's house
To share his needs
One man's boat
To sail the seas

One man, one house, one boat

One man doesn't have to live alone
One woman can share his throne
One woman can be
His precious stone

One man, one house, one boat

One woman to give and share
One man to know she really cares
Kindness, love, sex & passion
Joy, compassion, & satisfaction

These are things that two can share
One man, one woman = one couple

Ordinary Day

It was an ordinary day in my ordinary life
Until
My alarm clock went off at 8 am.
Why did I even set that darn alarm
I had no job to go to or schedule to keep.
Walking to the sink to get a glass of water,
My mind started to wander
It was way too early to be awake
The act of filling the clear glass
With water pouring out of the tap
From my kitchen sink
Into the glass seemed like such a chore
I started thinking, not about the glass
But where did this water flow from?
Where was the source?
It got me thinking.

Ordinary Woman

I'm just an ordinary woman
Nothing extraordinary
Just plain ordinary

I did what was necessary to survive
My poor beginnings
Were only poor for lack of the dollar

Instead
I was gifted with natural surroundings
That nature provided
Things like clean water, clean air
Breathing peaceful surroundings
Enough food to satisfy
Making me appreciate
The thing that sets me apart

I'm just an ordinary woman
Working hard to create
Something extraordinary
I never give up
I keep on creating
A better version of myself

I'm not legendary
Not living extraordinary
I'm just here
Living life

My beat beginnings
Have only forced me
To redefine the word Beat
Which to me means to keep evolving

Our Lives Have Turned

Our lives have turned into a big empty box. There once was a time when it was full. Full of Friendship, companionship, love, romance. All those things filled the box. Through the years things started to disappear. I tried to replace those elements, you kept pushing those things aside.
I may not be the best looking, the smartest, or have a perfect body, but I deserve to give love and receive love in return, just like anybody else. At times I feel so alone, I could scream, but I don't. No one is listening anyway.

Most people get married believing a myth that marriage is a beautiful box full of all the things they have longed for. At the start it's an empty box, you must put something in before you can take anything out. There is no love in marriage, love is in people, and people put love in marriage. There is no romance in marriage, you have to infuse it into your marriage. A couple must learn the art, and form the habit of giving, loving, serving, praising, of keeping the box full. If you take out more than you put in, the box will remain empty.

I've always wondered why people think everyone else is having a problem but as long as you are silent they refuse to see there is one. I must ask, "Are people so content with complaining about politics, our education system, their neighbors, all the woes of the world. That they can't show a little compassion to those in front of their own face?

Our Two Eyes Met

Our two eyes met
I saw a soul
I recognize from long ago.
We are not strangers though we just met
Lost from worlds past
We now connect.
What connected us, meeting for the first time?
Was it a look or a feeling?
How do you recognize a familiar soul?
I would have to say
I felt it, but saw it in your eyes.
I do not want to lose you again
But how do I claim you?
I don't even know your name
Do you feel the same?
How many lifetimes did we spend together?
I do not know.
Our two eyes met
I saw a soul
I recognize from long ago.
You seem to recognize me too.
You smiled and are approaching.
Maybe the connection is never broken just delayed.
All I know is a feeling.
Whether it's cosmic or earthly,
I will explore you, my new and old friend.

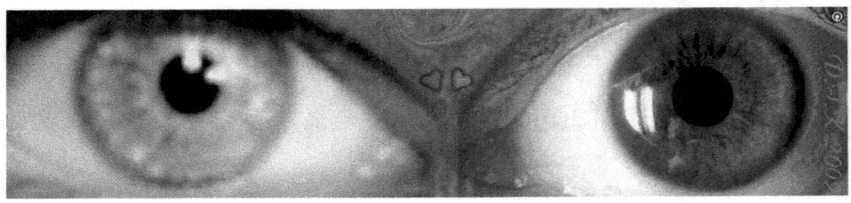

Passion's Muse

Silken skin
Passions thrust
Flames too hot
For human touch
Feast your eyes
On souls desire
Raw emotions
Set on fire

Sultry eyes
Silken tresses
Juicy breasts
Command caress

Dark wet thoughts
One must confess
Knotted ropes
Bound tight
Distressed

Lace and leather
Frees them all
For those who
Choose passion
Demand satisfaction

Everything you do
Requires passion
Passion leads
To sexual satisfaction

Spread your Love
Live your passion
Create a life filled
With satisfaction

Pure Bliss

Touching you
Kissing you
Feeling you
To your depth

Caressing you
Your emotions
The thought of us
Pure bliss

Peeling Apart

Our world is peeling apart
The lies of our youth are being exposed

We can no longer ignore
That we are living a limited life

No longer can we rely on the history books
To tell us fables

Instead we can embrace
Each other
Our pain
Our past

We can be better
We no longer have to listen
To the lies
The excuses

We are no longer ignorant
To the ways of our ancestors

Let's move forward
A revolution of evolution

The world is watching
I'm watching
Are you watching?

Are you with us?
Because We Are US
All of US

It's a person
Its' people
A group of people
US

Yes our world is peeling apart
It's exposing the truth
But also a new way
A better way

More love
More understanding
More unity
For US

Photographic Dreams

Dreams
Do not expire
They flutter through time
With never ending desire

Flashing past
In a blink of an eye
Like undeveloped film
Never printing the photograph

Dreamweaver's
Visionaries with creative souls
Open minded champions
Of the underdog
Seeing only the best in others

Dreams & Dreamweaver's
Floundering through time
Trying to find
Depth of perception

Looking through
Wide angle lenses
Shuttering through life
Giving a revelatory feel
As one compliments the other

Poets are Prisoners

Poets are prisoners
Practitioners, commissioners &
Conditioners of the spoken word

Caged by their own minds
Words are shackles
Holding poets' hostage

Puzzle

Looking out
Looking in
Can't find it
Empty of fulfillment

That thin puzzle piece
That fits the mold
Carried swiftly
You make it whole

Instead a mess
Of torn up pieces
Shredded bone
Distressed
Feeling alone

Just one thin piece
Missing from view
Don't know what to do
Living without you

Could find another
Twist it, turn it
Force it into place

But there is only one piece
That makes it whole

Queen of the Ballerinas

Did you really think I could forget?
The incredible canvas of pastel colors
With muted shades of pink
Intertwined with shades of grey
Allowing me to see
Beyond time itself
Within your eyes

Love is the greatest of pains.
I'm a Giselle
Whose straps have come undone,
Propelling me to dance
To the depths
Of a bottomless chasm,
Like Hell in Autumn

How could I foretell a future
Without you by my side
Our love, now portrayed
In a picture frame

Memories should start to fade
But...
You loved me too well.
Or did you love me at all?

Comparing myself to all before me
Realizing it was just a dance

Art imitating life

You, practicing your skill

Setting me to perform
Intricate moves
Into an endless Pirouette

Love shouldn't be a contest
As to how many turns you can make

You Loved Me Too Well
No, the truth is.
You didn't love me well enough.

Reluctant Soldier

It's a number
You always wished to be
Top dog
Number 1
First in your class

To most it seems
Like a good thing
A sign of honor
Ahead of the rest
One of the best

But now that number
Brings fear to your heart

You stand armed
At the front
Alone as one
Who fears the unknown

You're the #1 enemy
First to be seen
Only to be recognized
As the first target

This is the one time
You're just one soldier
A person who's number identifies
You as willing to be first to die

An honor for some
For you must fight

Hoping to survive
To be first
To return home

Remember

In a time when the future seems too distant to grasp

When your heart beats erratically

When those around you have lost their way

Remember

No matter your fate
You control nothing
Eternity is the only common destiny

Your submission
Is your acquiescence
To a sphere of contention

Which will bring you unity
In opposition

Grasp it
Then release it

Because nothing
Is something
And something
Is everything

Reminds Me of a Time

The lonely Merganser's call
Through mist covered paths

Reminds me of a time
Two beneath the native blanket lay

Wrapped in silence
No need for words
Feelings in a glance
Conveyed through a touch
Rippling waters of the river
Caressed our brows
As the eye of time
Watched over our souls

Reminds me of a time
Two beneath the native blanket lay

Revolutionary

I've been acquiesced
To be a revolutionary
In spite of myself

I never thought
I'd start a revolution
In a world of turmoil

Instead I envisioned
Myself as sympathetic
Taking in the ones
In the know
The ones whose words
Do not matter to most
But touch everyone

Instead
What happened was an evolution
A generation known
Using the ways of those
Whose words were not accepted
By those who follow the norm.

A new generation
An evolution of plain words
Sparking a flurry of excitement

The words mattered
The words brought voices
Voices that were told to be silent

The words sometimes inspired
An array of beats
Speaking music of cooperation
Inclusion of every shade
Notes of kindness
A new Beat Generation

Leading this beat evolution
Was someone who didn't want fame
Didn't want the spotlight

No! In fact she wanted only
To give everyone a voice
To include instead of omit

I found myself
Picking up the reins
And leading the pack

I started a
Beat Generation Evolution

Roots

Roots dig deep
Limbs spread wide
Living life as if in stride
Fruits they fall
Branches weep
Teary eyed
I fall to sleep
Denied, twisted, broken, frail
Fallen by the long lost trail
Beaten, cheated,
Freedom lost
Roots dig deep
Despite my loss

Sacred

The sacred flow
Taken advantage of
Turned brown & muddy
Poisoning all that drink from its source
Now oily with decay

What used to be cool, crisp & clean
Freely giving life
Nourishing all with its drops
Can no longer sustain it

Cannot fight against those
Making a fracking fucking dollar

Long ago In stories told
The Lorax warned us
To speak for those without voices
To shout out loud
Or be drowned
In a cesspool of waste

No one paid attention
As most do not now
It seemed only a children's story
A fable to read aloud

We all share this planet
It's beauty and wonders

Without a home
Where clean air & water rein
Where we no longer are free

We will be fracked to death

It's up to us now
We must fight and take a stand
To protect not only ourselves
But our brothers & sisters on other lands

For life giving waters are sacred to all
You can't drink life out of an oil can
Give a fuck & don't let them frack

Sad Turtle

Speak to the Beat of the Sad Turtle
It's shell now empty
Where only it's spirit resides

Once it was full of life
Its shell
Vibrantly colorful
With hues of orange and red

It rambled through forests
Swam in pools

Its favorite food was slugs
Although hard for it to catch

It dug in dirt
To lay its eggs
In hopes of a new generation to emerge

Now all that's left is an empty shell
As a reminder of the joy
Of a life that once lived
And the sadness of loss

Speak to the Beat of the Sad Turtle
It's shell now empty
Where only its spirit resides

Sadness Runs Deep

Like a river that feeds an empty well
Sadness runs deep within my soul

Smiling and laughing in the face of adversity
Inside withering like a tree sheds its leaves in the fall

Sadness runs deep within my soul
Like a river that feeds an empty well

Appearing completely without cares
While nervously awaiting a viper's strike

Like a river that feeds an empty well
Sadness runs deep within my soul

Laughing and joking in crowds around town
The person that people gather around

Sadness runs deep within my soul
Like a river that feeds an empty well

Warm and engaging to the people surrounding
Inside cold, like snow in the dead of winter

Like a river that feeds an empty well
Sadness runs deep within my soul

Like a full moon at its splendorous end
As it bows to deformity

Sadness runs deep within my soul

Scars Unseen

Outwardly, she looked fine
No bruises could you find

But beyond her sad eyes
Well defined & outlined

Emotional & Verbal abuse
It Leaves scars, YES IT DOES!

Creates a life full of stress
Crippled by years full of tears

Of cruel demeaning words
Feeling no one cares

Robbed of self worth
She wept, silently, alone

Said she wasn't smart enough
A moron, an idiot, stupid

Nothing could be done
To his satisfaction

Her feelings and desires
Just didn't matter

Afraid of his displeasure
She felt less than lesser

Her self esteem gone
Under extreme pressure

Now withdrawn
She lived in isolation

Demeaning her every word
His pleasure was to create terror
Find her every error

Years of living cut off
From family, friends
Her misery and despair
Took her mind elsewhere

Wanting to escape
But left alone
To stare at the walls

She dreamt of somewhere
A life free of strife
She longed to be
Free & whole again

It took all she had
To break loose of
The invisible chains
Created by her suppressor
And to finally leave

Those scars unseen?
Looking in a mirror
She saw a reflection
Of whom she wasn't
But had become
It made her see the light

She COULD have a life
Claim her OWN ideas

At peace
To finally be herself

Standing strong
She was worthy
As we all are

Emotional & verbal abuse
It leaves scars, YES IT DOES!

It takes love, love of self
To be proud of
To live a life of
Just being yourself

Scruffy

Flowers with scruffy lavender heads
Smiling shyly as the sun shines down
Giving them a warm sweet kiss
Their leaves twisting gently
Swaying in the wind
As if to pose for a photograph
Their tall green tendrils
Roots; burrowing into the rich dark soil
Spreading their roots in all directions
Making sure they hold fast
In case admirers were to want
To possess them
Looking up towards the sky
I look deeply inward
Pondering
While hoping to find answers
To life's most perplexing questions

Sea of Emotions

Zipping through my mind

A sea of emotions
Mental stimulations
Physical expectations
Surging jubilations

A sea of emotions

Numbed soul
Curled into a ball
Quietly struggling

A sea of emotions

Tender love
Flew off like a dove
Has broken wings

A sea of emotions

Unable to fly
Both the bird and I
Will most likely die

A sea of emotions

Loss of passion
Settling for less
No satisfaction
Stressed reaction

A sea of emotions

Shoe Whore

My first recollection was going to Grandma's
showing her my shiny black patent leathers.
In Winter I pulled on my bright red rubber water-
proofs securing the button loops.
Summer brought Keds, white, blue stripe-edged,
pink ballet slippers then taps.
Each new school year we visited the bulldog for a
pair of Buster Browns.
I guess when I think back,
I realize my parents were in fact, shoe whores.
They always blame the parents but in this case the
shoe fits.
They each owned scores of shoes for every occa-
sion, season, and for no apparent reason.
I thought every kid got a shoehorn in their stocking.
I had dance, bowling, riding, tennis, softball, hiking,
school shoes,
Just to name a few.
A pair for every outfit, weather,
And to brag to the neighbors that
Even though we were poor dairy farmers,
We could afford the finest leather charmers.
Later in life when my husband took me as his wife,
he started noticing small rectangular boxes.
Dress shoes, walking shoes, boat shoes, low heels,
high heels, hiking boots, thigh-highs, multi straps,
plaids,
solids, stripes, glittered, Mary Janes named after my
aunt.
I inadvertently and with certainty passed the shoe
gene to my son,
Who has more pairs than his wife.

I never even realized until given the exercise,
Of writing a poem with the prompt "Shoes"
That I was a shoe whore too.

Show Pony

When Show Pony puts on a show
People dish out the dough
Show Pony never disappoints
She smiles and prances
Bows and does dances
As the crowd wows her every move
Everyone approves as she kicks up her hooves
Cameras flash and she poses
People surely want a picture
Show Pony is a mixture
Of flattery and finery quite unique
After the show she takes off her bows
She's now a Plain Pony
Inside still the same
Same pony, same name
Yet no one gathers around
She is quite the letdown
Plain Ponies don't astound
She cries and is lonely
Feeling wounded, not included
No one seems to care about the pony herself
They just wanted to be a part of the Show

Silly

Silly I thought someone like you
Would want someone like me
You seemed to like our times together
We were happy you and I
As time passed you smiled less
Your touch was no longer sincere
Silly someone like me
Would think someone like you
Would want me

So Much Lost

So much lost

For some
Life

For others
A part of themselves

Both
Never to be regained

Only a memory of
So much lost

So Wonderful

So wonderful
So loyal
So true
Such a pleasure to know you

What is it that makes you
The person so revered
Never doubted
Nor feared

People trust you with their lives
So loved by all

Only at the end of the day
When the others go home
to their loved ones

You are left to enjoy
all the praise alone

All the praise and flattery
Doesn't help settle the soul
All the love talked about
Needs to be shown and shared
In order to feel appreciated
And not feel alone

So that's why the person revered
by so many
Feels alone in their glory

Stressed Heart

Stressed heart
Thought I passed the test
Not that I ever got rest
Eyes fluttering half asleep
Feeling skin deep
Stressed heart
Broken apart
Eyes see inside me
Hidden under a tree
There are two sides of me
Stressed to the max
Not up to the task
Stressed heart is all that is left
To bind me

Take Us Over

You clean up well
Your gait entices me
As you approach
Your scent fills my nostrils
I breathe your essence
My heart beats faster
My pupils dilate
Sweat beads surface on my skin
I'm warm and moist
You have penetrated my senses
You have excited my depth
Mutual feelings of desire
Take us over
This night is an inferno
Our fires are stoked
We melt into one

The Cost

My broken Heart
Shattered Soul
I've lost my way
Without your glow

Without you
To guide my way
No direction
Come what may

My broken Heart
Shattered Soul
Has left me lost
Without your glow

The cost for you
Not to stay
Has cost me
To lose my way

The Door

I am the door.
The door provides but you must provide the words
to open it.

The open sesame lingo that will charm
The masses to wanna hear those words.

The door has remained closed until now.
You spoke bullshit and the door noticed.

Only those with an open heart that speak of love, not
money, will enter this realm.

The door will set you free. It will transform you into a
loving, giving being.

Don't lock the door. Let it remain open to truth, to
kindness, to love.

The Expression of Me

The eyes tell all
Sadness, gladness

A picture
Tells the story
An expression of me

The camera captured
Revealed all

What sorrow could be
To make me feel
Empty, dull

Beyond words
Too dark to see

Far from touch
Lost without
No hope will there be

The eyes tell all
Sadness, no gladness

This picture
Tells the sad story
A reflection of me

The Forest is Many Things

The forest is many things

The sun filtering through the canopy
Creating a ambiance of warmth

The fronds of a fern
Curling tightly into a ball
As dewdrops lay upon it

But as nightfall descends
Shadows aren't always what they seem

Trees stay silent so others can be heard
Songbirds lay in their nests up high
Singing their songs softly
As they fall into slumber

Frogs chirp in unison
As fog creeps in
Providing them cover from predators

An owl silently descends upon an unsuspecting meadow vole
Who becomes sustenance for its young

A family of deer walks slowly
To the river bank for a drink

A skunk waves it's perfume
To keep others at bay
While it digs the soil for grubs

For some it is their home
For others a meditation
A contemplative peaceful place

Sometimes beautiful
Sometimes brutal

The forest has beauty as well as ominous tones

I wish for the forest to continue
Undisturbed by those who destroy its peace and its purpose

The Pounding Beat

The pounding beat reverberates
Like time echoes throughout my mind

Twisting and contorting my brain
Pounding it like a melon being beaten with a mallet

With no outside visuals
Words have been used
As virtual weapons to defeat and bring me down
Piercing my veins with their venom
Infusing me with thoughts of hopelessness

Broken and defeated is how the world wants it
Determined to dash my hopes and silence my heart

Emotions run rampant
Building up inside like a pressure cooker ready to explode into a Frenzy of confetti-like brain matter
But if you listen carefully to the rhythms, those constant beats spell out, "Freedom"
To lift this underdog to the forefront
Giving me strength when nothing else is left

The Real Thing

Others only dream of this
The realm of locked lips kiss
You can't keep them apart
The real thing
Bodies slipping between sheets
Sweets of desire like no other
Secrets shared while swaying in motion
The real thing
Merging and surging Into one
Never to part as time stands as one
Ascending into a converging refill
The real thing
What can be said of this
The rumor of a midnight kiss
Soft bodies both held in bliss

The real thing

The Search for Meaning Starts with You

The search for meaning in your life
Is not a solitary journey of one.
It starts with you reaching beyond yourself.
Seeing yourself in others you meet.
Look closely at your neighbor, don't turn away.
Embrace them with loving acceptance.
Celebrate every piece of beauty and flaw
outside and within.
Don't compare others to anyone else.
We are all unique yet the same.
They need not be human
for you to see these similarities.
Only when you recognize that each soul you meet
provides you with a gift;
Whether seen or unseen, will you grow to become
one with the world.
Journey forth and find your meaning in each and
everyone's life.
Only then will you find that you were meant to give
love, receive love, and be love.
The one true meaning in life is love.
You can't see it, you can't touch it. You can only feel
the light of it.
Find meaning in your own life,
just by recognizing that fact.

The Silence

The silence
Can you hear it
No you can't
It is deafening
There are no words
Just the void
There should be talk
The silence
Do you hear me
No you can't
I never existed
The silence
I am nothing
no one
I cannot be heard
The silence

The Silence Chimed

The silence chimed
As the first snowflake of the season
Began its descent

It came alone
To scout the territory

I watched In amazement
Its twirling multi-dimensional dance
A chiming bell of beauty with wings

It flittered silently past me
Sticking softly to the earth

Then the parade started
I often venture outside
To wait in silence
To witness this army of twirling dancers
Descending

They make a sound
Like the chiming of a faint bell
As they float in the darkness

At first I feel alone
As they have each other
They unite and gather
Forming a carpet of light

I stand to witness their unity
As their numbers increase

They begin to envelop me
Each one ever so gently
Laying their hands on me

It's a healing, nurturing act
Some on my hair forming a hat
Others melting into my bare skin
Moistening my spirit

They aren't just snowflakes
They are nurturers
Bringing sustenance
And hope
For the future

The Sun Shines

The rays of the sun shine upon you
You don't feel it as I do
I still walk upon the earth
You lie beneath it
I still breathe the air into my lungs
Yours no longer expand to life
The only thing not making me sad is
The thought that you are the rays
Streaming down upon me
Enveloping me in your warmth
Your light shines bright still

Thinking Of You

Sweet grass smudges
Can't free me
Of the sleepless nights
I spend
Thinking of you

Walking beaches
Sands are seamless
Waves seem endless

Pieces of shell fragments
Beneath the ocean floor
Where my mind wanders like waters
Dreaming of you

Strands of hair
Braided like filaments of memories
I bathe in reverie of you

Three Trees on the Farmington River

Three trees whisper
The ancient wisdom
Through the ages

Yet we do not hear

Their poems swirling
Upward through
Branches in the wind

Be still in their presence
So you too will hear

Time

It was 10am. I was working the day shift at the Kerouac Cafe & Bookstore. Not many people read books anymore, especially poetry books. They also have no use for people most of the time, unless they can use them for some reason or another.

As I sat on an old piano stool that had been there since the beginning of time, long after the old player piano had been sold and taken away by antique dealers,

I started to watch the expressions of people passing by the front plate glass window. I was positioned in such a way that I could see everyone passing by on the sidewalk, but also beyond that. I saw passengers faces riding by in the cars on the street too. Some sad, some glad, some looking like they were moderately mad.

There was one cute little brown eyed girl clutching her dolly and laughing at what her dolly seemed to say. People are funny creatures. They won't give you the time of day. They are rushing to get to nowhere. Worried they will miss something, yet, they don't know what that something is. Most look determined to reach a certain destination.

They have no time to stop in the cafe & bookstore, grab a cup of Joe, indulge in a little conversation, read some spontaneous prose. In the Kerouac Cafe & Bookstore we have some real smooth jazz playing in the background.

Me?

I take my coffee black and when no one's looking, I may sneak a tiny drop or two of fine Bourbon in there just for flavor. I've read all the books in this place, listened to the extensive collection of jazz available here.

I'm a thinker. I ponder the reasons why I'm here, where Ive been, where I'll go next.

I used to make plans for a life. I was just like one of those poor souls outside rushing to nowhere.

Time is cruel. It passes quickly just as the people do in your life. I've determined there's no time worth the time it takes to love someone.

I used to look forward to seeing my love, rushing to meet them. There weren't enough hours in a day to spend. In summer we used to go on little picnics in the woods, lying on a fuzzy old blanket, looking lovingly at each other.

Once a little bird perched above us on a branch, watching us entwined in each other's embrace. The bird flew away just as my love did.

Life is lonely now. I sit on this old piano stool, listening to sad music, sipping tainted coffee, staring out a window, watching people pass me by. Time ticks away, waiting for no one.

Tight

Hold me tight
Make love to me all night
I won't put up a fight
Come fly with me tonight

Today

Some of us didn't make it today
No matter how much you try to wish
The horrible thought of that fact away
No matter how much you pray
The feeling of loss
Just won't go away

If you look around
He or she won't be found

They passed away
Their breath consumed
A virus so efficient
They all were doomed

Their lives so important to the living
Now left behind to mourn

For some of us
We die a little each day
Trying to numb our feelings
Wash sorrows away

Some of us won't make it through the day
For others we'll get to stay

It's important to remember
What makes life worth living
It's Love

Making our time here
Whether a minute or millennium

Bearable

Some of us didn't make it today
But for those that did
Tell someone you love them
Today

Tragic Artist

Yes, a tragic artist
That's me
Molding the clay
Tearing pieces away
Painting on canvas
Messing with brushes
Ruining creations
On a daily basis
Drinking to excess
Of course showing distress
Yes, a tragic artist
That's me
Taking breathtaking photos
Of everything lively
While deep inside
Contemplating suicide
Ready to jump
What's the use of trying?
Down in a slump
Yes, a tragic artist
That's me
Creating beauty for everyone's eyes
But no one else sees
The tragic artist that is me

Travels Through Time

Through portals of time
Traveling to a place
A stranger's glance
An inquiry of introduction
Shyly smiling
We say our names
A spark ignited
Strangers no more
From that day forward
True friendship forged

No more loneliness
Someone to count on
Shoulders to lean on
Squeezed tight
Embraced with a hug

Years pass
As time travelers move forward
Until one day
Clocks pause
While true friends
Share stories

An unexpected reaction
A first kiss
Turns to unleashed passion

Time stands still
The sands sifting
Between friends
Now lovers
Till the end of time

Trees

Time floats through bare trees limbs,
As whispering winds change direction.

Willows draw water and rays
When offered nourishment

Maples tapped
Syrup flows into sweet nectar

Evergreens alive,
unchanged throughout seasons

Oaks tall,
branches flail to tell the tale

Trees silent,
sentinels of life's timeless journey.

Turtle of Despair

Eternally withdrawn
Unable to shed
The shell that surrounds me
So hard and rigid
Impenetrable to most

As time goes by
You can see my age
Counting the scales
Formed
By passing through forests
Diving down river bottoms
Sifting through sand

No choices
To where home is
Instead I carry it
As a heavy burdensome stone
Surrounding me

It's been this way for eternity
No one knows why
Causing me to be called
The Turtle of Despair

Two People

Two bodies
Naked
Exposed

Two hearts
Beating
As one

Two lips
Locked
In a kiss

Two eyes
Viewing
The other's soul

No status
No political affiliation
Nothing but

Two people
At that moment
In time

Just two people
Nothing else
But Love

Under The Stars

You could hear the tender waves
Lapping against the shore
Under the stars
The moonlight bathed our bodies
Our skin glistened against the motion
Under the stars
Our lips found their way in the shadows
Floating across the water
Under the stars
Consumed by the illusion
Of earth and sky merging
Under the stars
Pausing to look up
stars twinkled with a smiling gaze
Under the stars
We made love
Under the stars

United

They're Trying To Take Away Our
Privacy
Vote
Freedom of the Press
Clean Water
Jobs
Food
Healthcare
Education
Friendships
Freedoms

They're Trying to Replace it with
Walls
More Taxes
Hunger
Poisoned Water
Hatred
Guns
Killing
Death
Division

They're trying to Leave us with
No Hope
No Peace
Sick
Defeated
Wounded
Divided
Dead

But We are Strong
We Have
Hope
Voices
Truth

We won't be Silenced
We're Staying Strong
Aware
Well Read
United
Educated
Free

We Are One
Together
We Shall Overcome

When We Were Whole

When we were whole
We took up space
Moving freely
Seen
Touched
Heard

Now we take up space
In a obstructive way
Moving through time
Unseen
Untouched
Unheard

Our images present to the world
Not us
We are a creation
Existing in a void
In between spaces floating
Particles squeezed into a screen
A virtual background
In time

Our 3D definition
Can't be pinned down
It floats
Our voices echo

We might be those who have passed
Images in a screen
Heard by turning up the volume

Enjoyed by listening
Not touching
We are fragments
Of memories

When we were whole

We were seen
Touched
Heard

We existed in real time
We were not a taped image
Looked at through multiple screens
In the void of space
In other dimensions

When we were whole
We were a mess
Guts
Blood
Spit

We had no appointment
In order to be seen
There was no way
To hide
Once you arrived

We stood on ground
We were inside
We dared to touch
To hug
To kiss

Our tears could be dried by another
Our imperfections could be seized
The blind could touch our textures
Feel our heat
Embrace our touch

When we were whole
We were

When You Think

When you want to be a part of something
Think you matter and plan for tomorrow's happy ending
But realize you're a part of nothing
Hidden away as the new day springs
Last on the list of possibilities
You are sent on your way
Midnight rendezvous are all that remain
Alone to ponder living another day
It hurts down deep inside
Cuts through your heart like a steak knife
The only solution that makes sense
Is to give up or to not think
For if you think too much about it
You're sure to deep six yourself

Who are the Lonely People?

Who are the lonely people?
Are they the quiet ones?
The ones that look into the distance as if waiting for the sun to rise while staring into the darkness?
Are they the ones that smile a fake smile to hide the hurts bestowed upon them?
Are they the clowns who act clumsy in order to make fun of their utter pain of wanting to connect?
The lonely people often are the ones found in a crowd, surrounded by many people.
If you are wondering why they choose the masses over the solitude, it's because in the crowd, they can hide the fact they are alone.
No one will recognize them there.

Why

Why do people cease to exist
A question for those living
Reason enough
For the ones
No longer in life
Expressions and feelings
Discarded and ignored
No one to communicate to
Why couldn't they listen
Did it take that much time
Out of a day
For a life to lose all
No one to love them
No one to care for
Today a turning point
Nothing but
Dreams taken
Emotions stirred
All hope gone
It may be all over
Yet the crying remains
An empty shell
Of a person
With no reasons
Instinct took over
One thing left to do
The past
An illusion
A future
Dissolved
No barriers left
Another ceased to exist today
Why

Worth Expressing

Music & Art
Expressions

Sights, Sounds
Vibrations

Nature & Photographs
Coloring memories

It's what makes life
Worth living

It's what makes love
Worth giving

It's what the soul needs
Worth expressing

You Baby You

I've traveled all over
Seen many a sunset
Met many people
But no matter where I go
One thing comes to my mind

You Baby! You!

You stick in my mind
Like a beautiful melody
Like biting into
A sweet juicy ripe peach
On a sweltering hot day

You Baby! You!

You're like a cool drink
I'd like to drink you down
Or splash in your waves
Let you rain down upon me

You Baby! you!

Like a perfect roll
I'd like to blow on your dice
No need for luck
As long as you're there

Nothing lasts forever
But when remembering
The best of times
One thing comes to my mind

You Baby! You!

You Can't Tell Your Heart

You can't tell your heart who to love
Your heart has feelings
Beyond time and space
You can stop your brain thinking
But your heart will still be beating
Reeling for its one true love
Your brain will make sense
While your heart silly nonsense
Your heart beats fast and irregular
When its true love's in sight
It will be out of sight
Analyze all you want
Keep the two apart
But you can't tell your heart who to love

Your Heart, My Home

I long to return
To my home, your heart

There doesn't seem to be
Any place I'd rather be

Without my home
I'm a drifter

No place
To rest my weary soul

There doesn't seem to be
Any place I'd rather be

Let me return
To where I belong

Your heart, my home

Your Love Is My Life

Your love is my life
You connect me
Like the strands of a spiders web
Stretching down to my core
Your love completes me
Like notes played on an instrument
With fingers reaching to a distant tune
Your love makes me smile
From my insides down to my toes
You tickle me with laughter
As you warm me to breathe
Your love is my life

Your Music Gives Me Life

Your music gives me life

As your waters rush inside me

Your voice instills a spark

To which others grow

Your caress moves along me

As the notes of your trumpet sound

Your music gives me life

As your rhythm shows your heart

You Ruined Me

You ruined me
That was not your intent, but still
You ruined me
I no longer see the world as I did
You opened me up to feel
I had closed the door to my feelings
It had been so long since I had felt deeply about anything
You ruined me
I now am open and alive yet
There is no one to return those feelings
You are gone
You ruined me
I am ready to explore my new found passion for life yet
I sit alone with only my thoughts of desire
Desire of feeling more love
Excited by the prospect of new sights and sounds
Craving a feeling of longing until next we meet
The rush of an elevated heartbeat
Pounding and throbbing outside my own body
Stimulated by the fear of the unknown
Desire to be feeling more love yet
You are gone
You ruined me

You Saved Me

You saved me
When no one else would
Your kind soul
Saw through my pain
You gave me hope
To go on living
You nurtured the best in me
I responded in kind
There were no solutions
But it made the road traveled
Easier
Interesting
Although you saved me first
I'd like to think I saved you too
We're all lonely people
Looking for a place to belong
Thank you for making life livable

Yuletide Spirit

Decking the halls with boughs of holly
While some feel jolly
Others melancholy

Raising a glass of good cheer
Warms the spirit
While singing a Yuletide lyric

Candles lit
On logs brown and gold
Gathering children to tell tales of old

Seems at this time of year
Makes one want to share
Wishing it went on
Throughout the year

Debbie Tosun Kilday

is a next generation Beat Poet, award winning published author, writer, nature photographer, illustrator, artist, and expert high-roller slot player.

Debbie is the owner/CEO of the "National Beat Poetry Foundation, Inc." (NBPF) (2016-Present), and its festivals & "New Generation Beat Publications"(2022-Present). She is also the owner of Kilday Krafts (1981-Present) Debbie is Special Events Director of the Connecticut Authors and Publishers Association, (CAPA) (2005-Present) She is a Past President of The Connecticut Authors and Publishers Association, (CAPA) (2014-2016).

How to contact Debbie & NBPF:

You can email Debbie at: NBPF15@GMAIL.COM
To learn more about the National Beat Poetry Foundation, Inc., learn about its festivals, Beat Poets Laureate, and how to get involved, go to our website:

NATIONALBEATPOETRYFOUNDATION.ORG

You can find Debbie Tosun Kilday & National Beat Poetry Foundation, Inc. on:
Facebook, Twitter, YouTube, Instagram, & Linked-In.

Debbie Tosun Kilday Books:

Author of, "No Limits: How I Beat The Slots" (2012) - Kilday Krafts & CreateSpace (now KDP)

Author of "Farmington River Reflections: My Photographic Journey & Meditations" (2012) - Kilday Krafts & Blurb Books

Author of "Tantric Love Suicide, A Poetry Collection" (2013) - Kilday Krafts

Author of "Wooden Branches: Leaf Tree Friends" (2012) - Kilday Krafts & Blurb Books

Author of "Whispers" (2020) - Local Gems Press

Author of "Amidst the Darkness" (2022) - Human Error Publishing

NBPF Book Titles:

"BE-AT" (2017) - Local Gems Press
"Beat-itude" (2018) - Local Gems Press

"We Are Beat" (2019) - Local Gems Press

"Goddess Festival Anthology" (2020) - Local Gems Press

"Beat Generation" (2020) - Local Gems Press

"Beat Generation Evolution" (2022) - Local Gems Press

"International Goddess Festival Anthology (2022) - New Generation Beat Publications

"National Beat Poetry Foundation & Friends Remembering Jack Kerouac On His 100th Birthday (3-12-2022)" - New Generation Beat Publications

NBPF Beat Laureate Book Titles:

Greek Crisis - Chryssa Velissariou - Local Gems Press

"Words 4 Sandwiches" - Paul Richmond - Local Gems Press

When Ice Burns - Annie Petrie Sauter - Local Gems Press

The New Protestaments - Daniel McTaggart - Local Gems Press

"Homers Margites or The Triumphant Fool (As Told To Carlo Parcelli)" - Local Gems Press

"Mothering and Othering" - Tammi Truax - Local Gems Press

"I Feed the Flames and the Flames Feed Me" George Wallace - Local Gems Press

"Reading the Signs" - Aprilia Zank - Local Gems Press

"Broken Silence" - Darlene Fernandez (DeeTruPoetry) - Local Gems Press

"Humility is Not the Name of a Strange Bird" - Bengt O Björklund" - Local Gems Press

"Walk on Water - Donna Allard - Local Gems Press

"Love Is An Howling Beast" - William F. DeVault - Local Gems Press

"As The Beat Generation slowly surely comes to be recognized as the most important group of poets and writers in the history of America, Debbie Tosun Kilday has given birth to a new Beat Generation. She is the guiding force for a new generation of Beat poets and writers, of all ages, who are waking to the realization that the creative imagination provides salvation from suicide, from death in life, by revealing that there are alternative paths to explore in this world, alternative paths that lead away from the mundane, the superficial, away from submission to a lethal mediocrity, alternative paths that open into the radiant river of alchemical fire called LIFE. Since history is the embodiment of "fear, reason, social convention, and tradition," visionary Debbie Tosun Kilday has made it her duty, her responsibility, her compelling creative urge to crack history's encrusted, iconostasic shell by invoking, through her words and life work, a new call to action. In her AMIDST THE DARKNESS she opens her heart and shares her personal journey of awakening. With heart felt gratitude I say Thank You!"

--Ron Whitehead, U.S. National Beat Poet Laureate

www.ingramcontent.com/pod-product-compliance
Lightning Source LLC
Chambersburg PA
CBHW071156160426
43196CB00011B/2102